# XOXO & Farts Harry the Heart

## By Holly Cook

# XOXO & Farts
# Harry the Heart

By Holly Cook

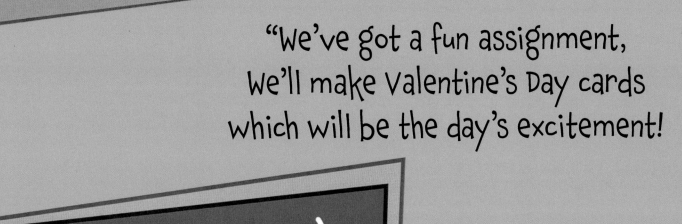
"We've got a fun assignment,
we'll make Valentine's Day cards
which will be the day's excitement!

Then the teacher said, "Let's share".

We all took turns so everyone could stare.

When it was my turn, I acted shyly.
I suffer from extreme anxiety, you see.

I began shaking and didn't know what to think.
My mouth was dry, all I could do was **BLINK**.

Then, I took a deep breath and said to myself
Being brave is good for my health.
So I opened my mouth and the words began to spill.
It was like I had taken a COURAGE PILL:

I FART too. That's why I understand.
Don't you know I'll always give you a hand?

There's so much in this world that causes worry.
Hope gas doesn't make you in a hurry.

When we can choose anything to be,
Why choose anything but happy?

Laughter and love is all I want for you.
And to find what you were brought in
this world to do.

It doesn't matter if that's playing games or reading.

Or even if it's just
FARTING, BURPING, or POOTING.

I accept you, stinky and all.

We could even go play ball.

No matter what the world says about you.

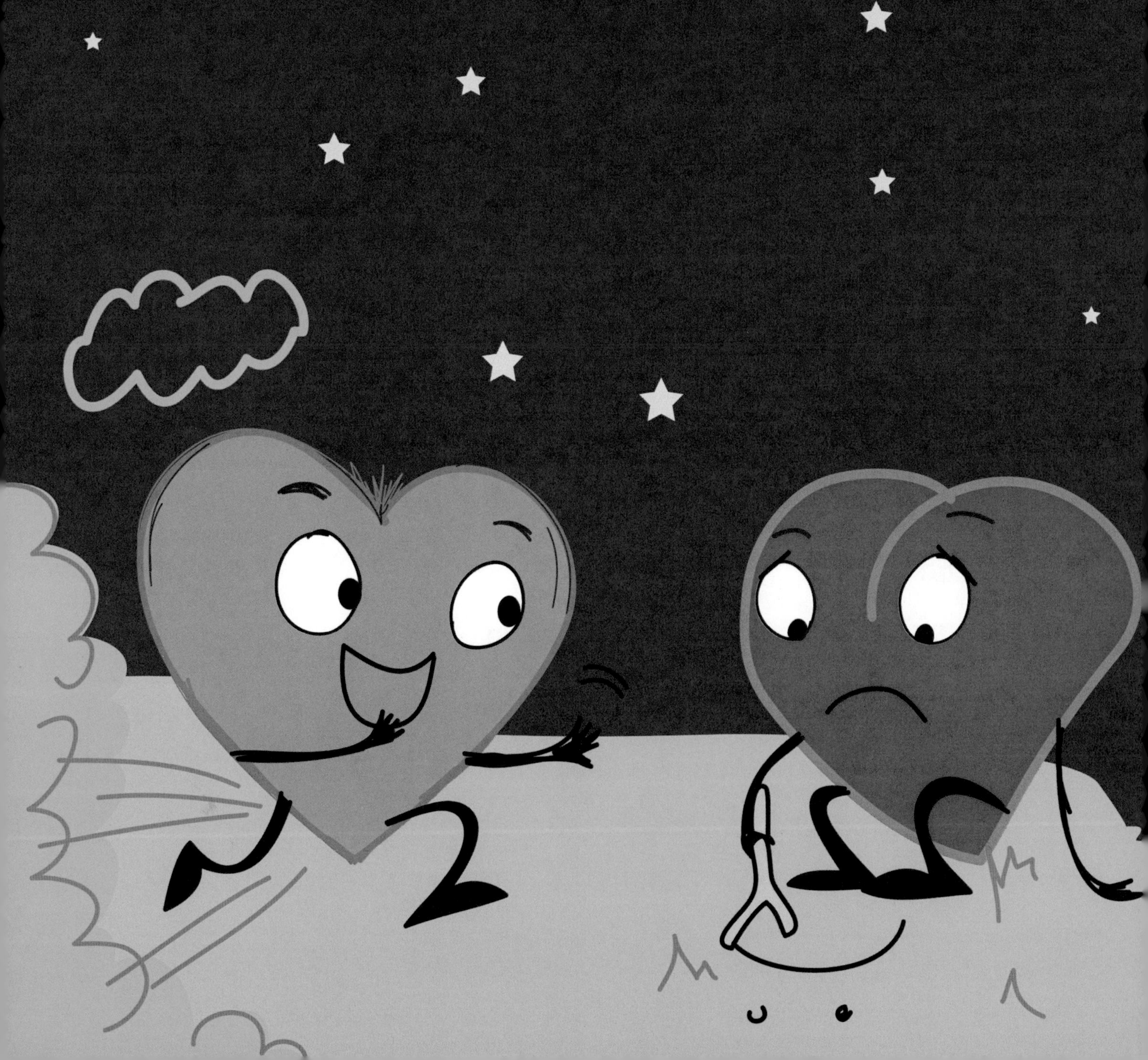

You're awesome, and they hadn't a clue.

Always follow your heart, and what it wants to do.

Take a moment to breathe, so
you won't feel **BLUE**.

Everyone poots, toots, and farts.

The End.

Made in the USA
Monee, IL
05 February 2023

27175168R00024